lloyd robson is a poet, performer, photographer, visual artist book designer, publisher, event promoter, w~~~ recovering journalist & all round ~~~

he has lived in cardiff, cwmb cardiff, plymouth & cardiff. h speaks with a stammer. for more dysfluency contact the british st ⌐ιαιιon, 15 old ford road, london, england, E2 9P⌐.

publications include 'letter from sissi',' edge territory', 'city & poems' (blackhat) & 'at the cairo café' - a poem engraved into the pavement on bute street as part of the cardiff bay arts trust public art programme. previously, he co-wrote with phil coles the south glamorgan health authority drugs education magazine 'the bizz' & was an early features editor for 'the scene' magazine in plymouth.

visual works include the 'sense of city road' photo-poetry montage, first exhibited on city road in cardiff, 2000.

PARTHIAN BOOKS

cardiff cut

lloyd robson

PARTHIAN BOOKS

Parthian Books
53 Colum Road
Cardiff
CF10 3EF
www.parthianbooks.co.uk

First published in 2001.
All rights reserved.
© lloyd robson
ISBN 1 902638 16 6

Typeset in foundry sans demi by NW.

Printed and bound by ColourBooks, Dublin,
Ireland.

The publishers would like to thank the Arts
Council of Wales for support in the
publication of this volume.

With support from the Parthian Collective.

Cover: design by matt jon
photography by lloyd robson

this is a period piece. it offers a 'factional'
version of cardiff at the
end of the twentieth century. in the time
since it was written some perceptions &
situations
(facts, public perceptions, instances,
circumstances, whatever)
may have changed.

A CIP catalogue record for this book is
available from the British Library.

This book is sold subject to the condition
that it shall not by way of trade or
otherwise be circulated without the
publisher's prior consent in any form of
binding or cover other than that in which it
is published and without a similar condition
being imposed on the subsequent
purchaser.

"behind the word
is chaos"

henry miller, tropic of cancer

"one thing should be clear...
ordering chaos is possible
only
by getting close to it"

joachim berendt, the jazz book

sunnyday but cold & slightwindy, gallopt inta town on the back
ofa cupa/bacon sarnie, turnd me ankle on corner of newport &
fitzalan, leaping out the way of a taxi. nasty stitch in the
bargain.

jumpt train wi no ticket as standard. rode the silverbrown
doublescore to newport, graveltrack run of quadruple scars
watchin steelbars curve soar curl across cities & moorland, via
splottbridge hundred yards from me own front door, but no
platform.

dock cranes & powerstat, transporter bridge & landfill site,
westbound train goes passt window, inches from me
glasssquasht nose in the corner of doorwell & toilet the
corridor someone askt if i've change but i'm distant.

newport:

& no one on door/checkin tickets; from station to subway &
the first thing to greet on this city street is the council
tax/benefits office, black glassfronted bars, solicitors, estate
agents

hit of fresh rain & deplete of sun; the redburn of clouds
stormwhipt from the door rush furnaces of llanwern; fumes
from corridors of trucks ghosting the M4 coalscab delivery
run/pavingslabs coming out of the sun/their cabs: mesht up; in
convoy

the westgate hotel

john frost square

gratis launch pissup: had me filla the grape, headed for a

rat&twat/pulld me escape, checkt out some bands: (coupla wets down me neck) softrockers *'ravensperm'* & locally renowned *'christstubble'*, what a double act, covers of traditionals with their own inimitable superthrash theological throat cack. get the crowd going mind. out.

drank up. considered parting the oceans but just one of the crowd taking part in the exodus up the street & city out. last thing i needs is the gospel bouncing round on a fridee nite for fucksake or - *sweet jesu* - crying out loud.

    ....

waiting at newportstat: two boys use a third to batterram the chocy slot gob the lot chuck the wrap at each others' heads, skate off to the end; take a spliff stop to ease the bones chill cable drone of temper rods befor they hiss & steam all over the platform.

headlow to take cardiff; catch the late again from paddington/the *'devonport royal dockyard'*, this territory chartered & homebound.

    ....

east cardiff:

(freightliner terminal: yellow travelling crane: bloke in the cabin: fag & the tellypage)

roath brook

rover way

white paint under splottbridge:

cardiff cut

'can't pay
won't pay'

'in emergency
press down the red handle'

inside the train.

✦

cardiff central destiny the thermovitrine keeps me warm & clean in carriage C; offers view in reflectovision as we reach the city. dribbling from stat into queues of orange buses into taxicabs & cityslabs dark, consumer durable & pissy.

> *'cold and tired*
> *pop in*
> *relax*
> *have a*
> *nice cool drink'*

> (windowpaint, spielothek amusement arcade,
> prince of wales theatre, st. mary street).

straight to the front of queue girls tryna get ina philly, lines of boys under lion canopy pissing their money over each others' shoes not a long sleeve between em not a goosebump let loose.

need food. consider a chinese but remember lastyear's poet in chowmein free-for-all incident/fraudulent use of/getting chased up the street. decide against it. settles for dorothy's fish bar in caroline street. cross & pass the shoepurmarket/taurus steak house/charlestons brasserie (an arc of chips surrounds a hit&run victim where caroline meets st. mary: not so much *cashed them in* as flung em each end of the zebra crossing). trudge the masses pisst up & in out up against wall of brains brewery: a mark of respect for the nite's liquid intake. otherwise known as recycling.

(the sweet response of a chipshop smile; the beauty of till girl reflects ina shine offa tiles)

orders currysauce & chips: when i eats when i'm pisst

everything tastes so superfuckinnatural so superchips so supertray so super plastic/wooden fork to throw away to catch under nails to remind me when i pick & flick in the morning; always a tossup between mayonnaise or currysauce depending on with whom you are eating. you gota consider tomorrow morning is what i'm saying.

(pause to eat; wipe curry from chops to me sleeve)

valleyboys hunting in brothers

scottish students lifting their sporrans & getting a barrel of cracks from the women

   "cold is it?"
        ("yack yack").

some girl tryna rid herself ofa beerbattered fortysumit mean preen sweatridden suitwearing *i am the man* divorcee: he clings like a pube to a telly screen; eyes everywhere, fingers everywhere; eyeballs on stubby fucking fingers all over her; she feels what he whispers thro teeth; eyeballs on claws makes her crawl deep out of reach he squeezes arms/narrows shoulders/presses tits into him/does not release, his moustache irritating her very existence her knees in that skirt: must be freezing.

this chromeshiny bigcity for the nite ladies man parading like *'the cardiff giant'* this oldster tryna pickup on studes & young mams in minis & hopefulness in sweatygrasp don't matter which to this tuftshufflin fuckin hasbeen as long as he gets within a mile of some pussy as long as he or she gets the wet hand duty tonite. both, preferably. jus doan tell his ex wife: he thinks she's still keen to come back to him.

a somali bloke throws his chips to the road & currysauce

splatters *the suit*'s shiny shoes which gives the woman
opportunity. the suit looks up at somali, sez something like

   "lick it up you scruffy cunt they're arfuckinmani"

the kardiffsomali sucks teeth & sez sumit to the effect of

      "splott market".

the girl last seen jumpt a taxi. alone to her kids.

   ....

               'this sunday
            live here at the king's
      something very new & entertaining
            THE OTHER WOMAN
            superb lesbian duo
         the very best in drag & cabaret'

         (the king's head gaybar public house & cabaret,
               corner of caroline street, sorry, *mill lane*
                  le quartier de euro cafés).

serenading from the corner: the biggest taff diva you ever saw,
or

      'cariadioli - the dame edna of wales'

as s/he's known universally & to whom the *Vale of Glam Organ*
holds a completely different meaning.

& the so-called straightboy labelqueens
don't realise they dress in drag to

𝄞 *purr leeeassse*

homogeneity

(kickers
 yves saint laurent
 ellesse)

witha coupla padded zebras tied to their feet costin a ton ata time well it's their fuckin money, adidas meself, if they're cheap.

✦

called to le citron noir: the el greco menu subject to control by market police, taxes & service charge (i am plain clothes inspector number fiftyfour: recently hadta shut down a '*beatles*' theme bar only opened that morning, i said as i left

"ya semolina pilchard was off"

they said as i left

   "you'er barred."

bloody ha, but the only one laffing was me when i made me report to another restaurateur name of aristo the greek top man to politicians he seeks to please, to grease. they were shut down as soon as the lab got a hold of what came out in me shit. but enough of the day job i'm here to meet...)

bloke barges straight after me & into the faces of two honeybees buzzing it up, screams at them

   *"romantic young loves!
   do not bring the furniture of divorced couples into
   your house!"*

& leaves with the help of a large kick up the arse. but he has a point & they drink to it; drink to him on the street.

at the bar i comes over all yankcop & orders screwdriver (vodka, o/j, angostura bitters), black russian (vodka, coke & tia maria), a pint of dark & a slippery nipple (sambuca & baileys); gets joined by a middleage shinyshirt victim orders himself a silver mercedes (vodka, champagne, orange & cranberry) & a peach schnapps in a bowl for his alsatian *southpaw*. this here's aristo dexter, aforementioned owner of this overpriced mixt med ponce joint & so called cos he takes it away with both hands. sez to me

"yasoo, i know you, is the herring still red? are the birds still blue? did that story get out or is my rep still smooth after my AHEM little indiscretion?"

"where you been? i been looking for you, may have a little work..."

i shrug & grin & avoid saying anything but my eyes

"ah but you don't miss much so here it is from the horse's mouth: our mutual friend will be leaving tonite. the story: our editor the enigmatic doctor truth caught up & put him onto that shitlist youth who can't be found down the bus station no more: let them think he's on the 'harry secombe' *outa town/better than the coldslab i carted him away in my own private ambivalence, tho he was in charge of the gas: figure that, but you know all this, true? tho i digress i am right - but tonite it all comes down so have your cameras primed cos meester big's gonna be pulling out & i think we need a final shot to get the red book ready for his* this is your life *& reel the fucker in/bring him down & if you'll pardon my french: pin the winkle out".*

the truth is i haven't a clue what the fuck he's on about; he gets involved but i avoid/occasionally run a few rolls/check his competitors now he thinks i'm in tune & knows

ALL

every plan's about,
but me: i'm just a convenient snapper on the dippyside of a double-edged mirror waiting for a pile of grubby fives for filming religious & political leaders getting it away with those who, in certain lights, could be referred to as *children*. but don't ask me to identify the miscreant visions cos fat sweaty arses all look the same to me.

& aristo, to be frank, is a cash&carry cunt who always buys life by the catering pack the metric tonne he wants it all; used to work with him on the donut stalls in the days when politics & religion first took hold of his sexual exploits when everything he did was in focus thro my lens, cos i was the only one who knew which end of a camera to point & where, then he got into massage parlours, sexshops & portrait studios, where their every sexual gesture was for him controlling measure an opportunity too good to miss to suck on the power juice of lofty men to bring down bishops & MPs or rather: he likes to keep with the grip & the grapple/his hook in the grist/within reach of the city gents; have a hold on them; to get a feel; to get a reel, a set of negs.

fuck knows why, i always jus thought him a dirty old twat but so what he pays me on time & time again. i tell him i'll get out there next morning.

"just make sure you remove the lens cap"

(how many times?)

"kampai"

"drink up"

"juss one more then"

*"one more then shift ya arse - i want results, i want
the negs"*

get him to order one last round & some substance is found in
the palm of my hand from a shake for reassuring my activities
continue. nip to the bog to examine contents, check face in the
mirror take one last look so i can remember later my attributes/
how i'm meant to look, & wash down one of these microdots
he's cookt up, put the remaining in me likkle levi's pocket like
that's not the first place the polizia would look, walk back to
the bar &

"efkaresto"

"tschüß"

out the door & into the cool nite.

....

commotion echostorming up the arcade from offduty CID &
rugbymen panelling random city youth stupid enough to be
out at nite *remind me of that sales pitch again?*

'it's brains you want'

o-ay,

never forget you're welsh.

the supre hombres, the mountain men, plainclothes & uniform:
too much neon sends them off the end.

(man they was donuts bar none, tho i soon learned to not go &

eat one: in the hole-making process many public figures had more than a hand, i have prints; i have negs; i have ammo...)

....

'the city of the grateful knights'

'like putting your hand in a bees' hive'

....

poster in pub window

'olga likes men'

(that's why she punches them out
& takes home to bed).

cardiff cut

✦

> *'& now my life has changed / in oh so many ways*
> *my independence seems to vanish / in the haze'*

hayes island:

> *'master gregory's*
> *outfitters for young men & boys'*

> *(this week only:*
> *cardigans with elbow patches sewn on*
> *dated: this year of our lord...)*

𝄞 *reeeleasssse mmeee*

security approaches with a 50p on his head: i takes his foto
then a detour (the camera: he don't know what to do; goes
giving eyeball instead).

& in the public convenience under *the haze* sits lockt a young
girl with the look on her face of a new welsh madonna; she sits
in a stable/a fluorescent lit cubicle her hands fold together her
head tilts an angle & her long olive nose, luminous tracky
trousers loose round her legs/down to her airsoles & takes
place the immaculate miscarriage: not a donkey in town, the
only star dissecting glassy cobbles above her upturned auric
crown, the orange nylon clashing with a bloodred stain, the
three blue stripes mirroring her veins, & deep the embryo
down takes multiflush long enough to hang around for her to
see it has her brother's face (childporn offenders hidden under
beds; neighbours outside dallying for head; out in the street

"*i just wanna be your friend, you can't sleep here, but i can give you a bed...*")

'cleanse the streets'

(neonleak streetlites were cheating me)

from hayes: avoid working & trinity; go round the rear.

calls to some hotpit hotel (the stainglass spirits were calling me); slide to the bar & snuck arm on the counter my elbow to beer the schlopp ofa tenna outa velcro wallet a pint of clout sensuous/chaser/packet of crisps

> *"change!*
> *thank you dear"*

take a seat. pub fulla tightcurl redhaired women (*ah! miss yumyum*) then realise mirrors. cheap mirrors.

scan pub: me eyes get stuck ona fruitmachine flashing out

'features or cash'

(the continuous dilemma: *'high stakes'/'big jackpot'*)

those lites always suck me round/me cash away gimme a pinball anyday (...memories of stopping at every little roadside caff in cyprus: a keo & change/a pile of coins/that's me for the day ...larnaca to lefkara home of lace, old blue rented austin maxi or allegro i forget which still righthand drive because of the british up countrydust roads up edge of mountains/island crust pinnacles, car overheats, leads to cliffhanging trek after miles of *longway up* on driver's side & *longway down* outa nearside, burst a tyre & it's sheer drop to a bunch of flowers & a spot on bbc world service radio ...meeting up with aristo the greek, him arranging a taxi/sixdoor automatic mercedes sweaty plastic vinyl seats/windows open & a poxy little fan on the dashboard the constant click of worrybeads for the remaining week ...ran him a few errands ...driving up to nicosia passport office in searing midday temperatures hanging round for hours to get a fuckin form stampt then back to larnaca head to head witha UN jeep, roadrage on behalf of the turks by the swedish blue bonnet bastards/the blond police ...getting the paperwork sorted ...swarms of birds around early warning station up in the troodos range ...dodging forces across the mediterrain ...flying out from akrotiri famagusta'd in the head ...flying back to britain & chucking up midair ...*ah the joys of our cypriot escapade*... unable to shake the cunt since...)

doors rush open to a groupa *jack* suits demanding a lock-in still on their lunch break their cheap shiny ties their can't be arsed shoes (this city welcome for refugees escaping somalia kosovo england ireland & swansea *O-ay: swansea* they enjoys their right to the nice house/job/surroundings but still not one good word for their capital lodgings *now what kinda welsh logic is that?* you don't like: get ya arse out, simple as that).

....

bloke approaches selling dutyfree. buy a packa gold V.

chopsymonks & monkeychops all over the pub like a job lot of speedin cartoon characters: *blahblah bunkbunk* monkeychops & chopsycunt stood in me lugs mouthin rave panza symbolism betting tips shag accounts whatever the fuck whatever smooth screw chat he/we comes out with like

   *"let's hit the kinky cariad clwb baybee
   i wanna live u up"*

yeh, to the fifty year barmaid; from the otherside

   "i'll give you seven to four that bloke starts a fight"

looking at me, but not meaning me. jus sizing me up.

in steps *chatty lang*. makes up his own mockney rhyming slang/sez to this bloke

22

"that's a big bottle you got there"

bloke looks & sez

"eh?"

to which chatty replies

"bottla gin: chin. get it? mate? eh?"

gets a bottle alright, & a face fulla stitches to straighten his grin.
well out of order if you want my opinion.

....

arguments amongst the clan

*"i seen him grow from a boy to a man & that's more than
she can ever say..."*

& whisperd from behind

"oi buggerlugs..."

some geezer lookin to sell me. substances offering subtitled
existence not substance but sex

*"step with me boy up to the harry o'tel, i've a harness you'll
find hard to beat, you'll discover you've a real man inside,
come up to my suite..."*

tell him to go home to his wife. & him a career priest

♪ *le-ett mee ggoooohhhh*

gess caught in the frontrow ofa ginrage catswirl between family; landlord goes nutta as they all do eventually, threatens to throw everyone out

　"ju nose wha i fink?"

pubs fulla dozy advice & plenty of people to offer it? i notice acid's kickt in so i'll juss sip at me beer/switch vision to colour/sit tight like a rivet in a bridge. it's difficult to tell the dancers from fists but tonite the contestants are antie & niece. the menfolk less pisst. for now at least

♪ *oooaaaaaghghh*

drink up & get on. could do witha burger bout now.

cardiff cut

rounda backa mArkzies: the brick of the wall warps out to me. see for yaself.

ata topa charles street: lucky jim's betting shop (lease for sale).

pisst white bloke wi dreds outside burgerking corner wi queen street, only noticed him after i'd been in, he's taken a kickin so i leans over/eats chips, dips one in me ketchup & waves it at him

"you're gonna need stitches mate"

he looksup at me, sez

   "u do us a fava mate ay...."

i buys him some skinny chips but deny him the chance to kip me settee. stomp off wondering what the welsh is for *taxi*, the police coming after me asking

"what did i see? nothing mate: me glasses: can't see a thing: the rain on the lenses bubbling the image, take a look for yourself: recognition unreliable to say the least"

& me praying that's not jus the acid doin its thing.

the copper hands me specs back, looks at me wearily, warns me as i walk away

   "there may be more questions so expect to be hearing from me..."

𝄞 *iiiiieeeeeeeee doan'tt*

𝄞 *waann chuuuuooo*

𝄞 *enn nee mooooaaarrrrrggh*

𝄞 **horh horh**

𝄞 *hor hor*

ringing up & down almost every street.

(there'ssssssjussssstooomuchhhhhovthisssssgoinrowwwwwnd,
gota get me arse outa town)

black man in a white robe stands preaching the word of his
lord to pisstup pedestrians. he gets told

    "yeh right mate, fuck off"

        in no uncertain terms then sees me, raises his arms
& his eyes to the skies as if in anticipation as if commanding the
stars & bellows in my face

    "you are being watched!"

       i see a caged van cruise slow & surveillance tv, look
from one to the other & do an imagined flickt vees, stride to
park place to get me a taxi, shouts back to the holy bloke

"sorry mate, no way is you scabbin a lift off me"

he gets approacht by the police while i tells drive to take me to

cardiff cut

clifton street. drive accelerates away & then turns to me

> *"tha cunt ina sandals: ad im in yur the other week, ad no muny, wanted me ta take im ta galilee - so i sez righ i sez: me not know way to gallery, but can take you to museum or art college, chop chop, velly solly!... fuckin laff? i felt like givin im a lift for free, yack yack, but fuck tha daft kunt, not ina back of MY fuckin taxi"*

yeh right mate. praise the lord for cabdriver charity.

we goes passt dylan's ignoring the fights, i gessa flashback from temping as a shirt&tie up early mornings & all that cleanshaven shite/flashback from when the place burnt out: flames hit a beautiful spring sky (i watched the building burn from a great height; watched firecrews from the topflight of the friary tower, looking down from pearl assurance welsh tallest building ta firemen hosing photograph posing yellowtops pivoting air, pissing on flames how it seems up here; greyfriar towa, municipal powa & look down lookt down city lunchtime topless burnin burning like a cherry flambé & the crowds the crowds all cheerin cheering

> *"go on! go on! burn the fucking lot down!"*

as real as the turin shroud i screamd we screamd

> *"burnit! burnit to the ground! go on my son go on!"*)

upfront the drive swears

> *"another fuckin one"*

> & finally shuts his mouth.

the rassclunk gearchange from second up to satdee, drive pulls an 8track from the pile on the passenger seat, 70's soul compilation blasts either side of me, along with

" : *four nine*"

                              " *four nine :* "

" : *where you to four nine?*"

" : *two two*"

                              " *two two :* "

" : *universal street to crystal avenue via wild gardens road*"

                              "*six four :* "

" : *six four: the sanctuary to watchet close*"

" : *five O* "

                              " *five O :* "

" : *bookem dano!*"

                              (*a torrent of abuse from five O*)

" : *keep yuhairon; station call from sanatorium road*"

                  (" : *scramble blue seven*")

" : *who's in town?*"

cardiff cut

" three three : "

" : three three: crockherbtown lane to roath dock road"

(neon & headlites flash thro the window).

....

sprayed under bridge to queen street station

'camraz suck satan's cock'.

....

little fridee blackdress stilettos in hand crosses newport road; from outside the blind institute towards west grove. drive eyes her up & ignores common sense/red lites/highway code almost slams in the back of an ambulance on slowmo/on its way to infirmary *(head injury, gotta be)*; slams anchors dead urgent & swears to me

"stupid kunt's problee dead by noww anyway"

(on the sounds: isley brothers' *who's that lady*).

needs must when the devil drives: i chucks ina back of iz taxi, hit his upholstery tho just miss me coat (*landslide* by tony clarke followed by johnny johnson's *blame it on the pony express* on the stereo) i coff up a lump out me throat

"one three : "

" : one three"

"he's chuckt in me friggin taxi : "

" : so charge & get rid of im"

" : three eight"

" three eight : "

*" : three eight to knox road.
park on the pavement under the wall. use your horn"*

" one nine : "

" : one nine: synchro city from newport road"

(synchro city:
   where everything is linkt

(synchro city:
   where there's no such thing as coincidence

(synchro city:
   a metropol in stasis a miserable fuck in constant crisis a
   weeping twat ofa town scabbed magnificence with saints &
   human garbage so why love it?

   becuz
   it fuckin askt for
   it deserved it.
   )))

   ....

drive's having a serious go so this time i chucks out the
window. liquidsplayed streets with a curry tint. drive pulls in,
drags me from cab outside splotlands pub & takes off down
meteor street. i stumble/swear/trip & fall/spill me guts & me
pockets all over the road & hit the ground anything but

running; can jus make out the remains of marvin's *what's going on* as i crumble in gutter.

....

misspelt declarations of love sprawl across sidewall of costcutter

'ramyond is lush'

further down: a derelict mattress lies burnt out.

otherside: moira terrace; a rack of beautiful almost amsterdam red & green wooden baywindows hang over street *(postcard, pure postcard, when they're sunny & clean a fresh lick of paint but defo very europeen)*, sweetwrapper trail for dangerous partners leads to women's aid beneath.

writ large on wall

'lenin lives'

(in st. peter's street)

....

take time to check one of the twin minimalist fire escapes behind GUM/west wing infirmary. further: the aerial-adorned crown of thorns pearl tower in distance. closer: the black&steel NPI building, zoom down the tap-shaped 60's chartered trust glassblock stolen from *tracey island* (the great crosscut from roath & adamsdown looking down westbound; the great architectural crosscut of kAAhd- from a kerbstone: the best place to view it/the best place to come from).

but the only one here to place value on money is the oldster up street tryna pickup a twenty a counterfeit glued to the floor. every penny's gracious but who's most susst: i got a free ride almost half way back while he has a dodgy score stuck on a slab. one thing's for sure: if i don't shift me arse we'll be here all nite, stuck on a kerbstone in a tarmac trance, the old bloke putting up the fight of his life against superglue & colourcopies & the humour of builders on site on the other side of planet street who done this to make everyone who passes think it's a wonderful life but looks a right twat. they caught me already. twice.

stand up. consider going mate's flat; spin round about turn & aim for city road/junction & traffic lites

& in the blue tinge of ambulance lites the inspection cover outside the CRI looks remarkably like the turin shroud: the folds burn out; its second mention of the nite. & lost below in the depths of that manhole tubular cameras lay jammed in the pipework abandoned to the wiles of sewage lines: worth thousands of pounds, i knows the man lost em that man was me dad now the A&E's shutting down ju reckon he'll ever get em back is he fuck as like

"oi ya fuckin cunts, gimme me fAth's fuckin camraz back!"

medics turn from the warmth of a meatwagon's insides, check out the gobby bloke, return to their rabbit & extralites, stuff like

> *"did you check out the rip on that fucker's face? pickt him up on tudor street - biggest one i ever seen since the roath/cathays curry war of 96, you could read a reverse 'sheffield' on his cleavered cheek for months afterward...".*

....

stop. rolla spliff ona wall, corner of newport & glossop opposite both CRI & city road/on rim of the church of st. james the great/on edge of surveillance tv. huntin dead lighters. my pocket a graveyard of ript rizla packets loose skins change snotty tissues & matches, penlids all that remain the bic's & biro's long lost to coat lining. spark up & stroll on. head down & up city road passt heron house income support office, east city hq

'the department for the concerned is shut today'

you can tell from the state of the doorway: a no smoking zone. when you're here the queue's not for clients' enquiries it's to sparkup & outa the wind. benefits unpaid & forms returned giro's not arrived & the staff upturned behind perspex & microphones away from the prams, perceived weirdos, & crews. emergency loans now required justa cover the cost of fags smokt while waiting ya turn (a sintax to punish prospective deviants dreaming of the chance to have their hands caught not so much *IN* the till as waving to it when it comes on the telly, so hurt them where it hurts: in the purse in the sack money goes where money knows so take a pill & get over it money knows where the party's at & it ain't in the queue for heron house in the fagends on the pavement slabs nor in the pocket of the dozy twat walking passt in the the vomit of nite desperately tryna remember how far to his mate's flat so he can raid his kitchen/his fridge/his plants, get his arse outa sight).

....

laffingman approaches: lungclaps punctuate halfjokes/don't wait for response/laffs to himself/never gets to the punch/he's off again: down the road *what the fuck is he on about?* fucknose, he's always like that from what i know; always on form.

snookerclubs: boys hang around with cues in hand waits for

the barman get off his fatarse check the screen release the catch & let them in. they're looking pretty smart: a private match, no beers for me in there tonite then.

....

reach mate's & buzz intercom; arrives late & reekina chips/beer/sick & mildly blitzed, greasefingering me pockets for a packet of skins & climbing the stairs without tumbling. inside flat there is much chaos, perversion & despair; no expense spared the margarine drips from floor to bread; the place is a shithole but the food from the licensed premise downstairs smells exquisite no less.

stick kettle on, build one, sit & stare, collect myself, take a wash & while i'm there nick a fingerprint of toothpaste to get rid of the taste from my taxi escapade. replace me hat&coat & go give me mate an A. he takes it from silverfoil & downs with his ale, puts down his glass & picks up a hammer from the side of his chair & goes behind settee where i'm sat, pulls out a brightly painted papier mâché fish which he places on the table, sez

"right ya cunt; watch out"

raises the hammer & pummels side of the fish down to nothingdust. i didn't pick up on as quick as i should/me feet propt on table flew from the wood, little bits of smithereen all over us

"fuck wha u doin!?"

but all is revealed: the belly fulla top quality marihuana flowerheads sown grown & flown over from south of the border deep down mexico way

34

cardiff cut

"our man in the americas; it arrived yesterday"

we unwrap with care, both rewrap in 3skin with energy;
anticipate the first blast arome when we open the packaging,
the address label markt

'*TNT*'

(goodnite vienna, sut mae synchro city...)

✦

hit spar for late shopping. queue at the grill. bloke at the front asks

"any milk?"

assistant takes his key out the till walks along counter lifts flap negotiates half empty boxes spilt packs down the end of the aisle to the cooler cabinets at the back of the store (we entertain ourselves while he's gone, hallucinogens & stripglow of spar), picks up a pinta fullfat & returns to the counter, walks to the grill sticks key in the till hands over carton & sez

"anything else sir?"

bloke sez

"i wanted skimmed"

the queue goes uproar: half ina rush to get home, half off their faces & pissing themselves as assistant has ta go thro it all over.

we gess chatting to the girls ahead. they wait as someone serves us (we order beer, bogroll, loaf of bread, disposable lighters, chocolate, rizla, cigarettes, O & a coupla porkpies: buffet size: all they had). the staff say

"enjoy yourselves/have fun/be safe"

knowing what they're selling & to whom & when (more than most of their customers aware; the girls on chocolate comedowns, the blokes grow impotent but too stoned to care).

girls in queue been drinking at angel hotel

cardiff cut

angel hotel: where norman bates was arrested for possession of cannabis posted from his missus in states; intercepted by customs & sent on its way; longhaul across atlantic for the sake of a setup fuh fucksake

the angel: where major major delivered a speech to the local representatives of the conservative party told them & the world how the city of cardiff was leading the united kingdom outa recession i mean: i still got an egg with his name on it

angel: where a student bumps into a bloke off the box, next thing: his wife declares frontpage disgust at the sight of his boxer shorts on a redtop bust

the angel: jus down from the toucan & canton bridge where washup south walians who've jumpt in pisst at the prospect of never finding work/love/their home/their feet *(the taff/ely/ newport usk: none of em can cope with the rush; if the tides don't get em crohn's disease will shut the poor fuckers up)*; barmy balmy nites crossing canton bridge into riverside/ überterritory across the city/self-proclaimed artists' quarter or *(fuckem)* muggers' paradise/sorry, not riverside, it's *pontcanna darhling*

the angel: over from the great shitbrain zoo where animals clamber walls/turn ta stone/attempt escape to the filthy orangefilter glow bouncing off shop panes/over the walls of citycastle into backalley deaths & towercranes above the arms park...

spermspew gardens of sophia; prozzies, arseholes, mounted police on undercover coming to the sound of car alarms, hotwires, helicopters flashing over head, handcuff & baton fuelled by a desire to put this youngbastard to bed...

a reservoir of effluent breaks its dam/bursts taff embankments, an orgasm uninterrupted by shitpushing dogs walkt by waterprooft wankers unaware of the parkbench shiftshank shafters of gaysex cardiff parks at nite, or maybe *aware*, that's why they go there: the loudest complaints from those who refuse to alter their route/cheapthrills for the righteous unaware it's their ilk who hide under moon & if unlucky: arrested: the zoo patrolled by titheaded horsefuckers riding beamfields/secret invasions litup & collared by legal uniform fetishists wank to a manjack of em; nocturnal promenaders kaarn av no privacy their individual wants trapt in public lavatories; agent provocateurs getting what they want themselves then arresting their young devotees, satisfaction no guarantee of freedom. but later released: the evidence didn't stick/still stuck in a copper's belly...

youngcocks prod holes in chipboard panels/names & numbers scrawl promised examples of secret lust (who's most disgusting lads: those who cottage or those who'd merrily beat the living fuck? it's pretty fuckin obvious: *you doan wanna suckysuck?* then wait til st. mary street where we're all allowed the pavement as lavatory/where a canvas lion guards against cockwatchers/scatmongers/police officers as we chuck, piss & punch streetsleepers/taxis/anything dulld enuf to hang long enuf ona bogstandard fridee nite down from the valleys, ready for the shuffling satdee shop crew who learn to shut their collective nose & mouth first thing in the morning. someone burn the lion out befor he sees too much. you have already. tidy. *whad? he look at you funny? hairy fuckin cunt...)*

the angel: the students in queue who invite us to party. O yeh. nice touch.

& the cheap beer claimed *'premier'* so we drank it while walking down street & up stairs to settee. prepare for the rest of eve tho by now it's deepnite, clearly.

cardiff cut

we return to the flat offload then repack & make off for miskin street. reach party & pull a smile to get in. there's an 'E' from a tesco's fallen in hall, problee nickt from albany.

frontroom:

congregation all denominations some leaning some fallen some risen some balling out how it is; some banging away like there's nothing at all to this to this life business raving like hyper speakers of makaton &

"get on"

to em all/dance away.

frontroom:

eye candy lushing up ona thousand kisses; hipster pants fulla shimmying women/huss cariads/spangled dubcats/discolites & synergetic visions in lycra *(i like-a)* but first

"where's the beer?"

the kitchen it is then; check the fridge.

i takes out & open a coupla cans & hand one to me mate. he's talking to the two girls who mentioned the place when we were down at the late shop. we chat, swap samples of what we have & separate knowing we will each provide the others with a friendly face throughout the nite catch sight of each others' glaze while we burn & blaze thro this sweaty throng our smokefilld lungs shouting out but forgetting names. the focus pull of recognition when we travel thro rooms/spill thro grin-bouncing dancers staircase sirens & long headnodding sessions ina backroom over homemade bongs buckets listening to dodgy rave tapes or - *christ help us* - an enthusiastic didgeridoo player who never stops for breath. house parties. hmm. the girls share their amphetamine crystal; we give em acid & mex.

two blokes other end of table handing over a rolldup note/lean over revolving yinyang breadboard/bending over/inhaling dust (someone tellem bread crumbs are not good for the lungs).

we go walking, settle on the stairs to see who comes in. then this weird thing between me & some local steel: group of lads at the door (i watch from the sixth or seventh stair) barge their way passt the host who opens expecting a porch fulla friendly firstyears, gets mobpresst instead by a gang of four dodgy looking crimjunkies off their heads; peers to make sure there ain't more of em coming & shuts door with stealth. he's stuck between door & the crew in the hall, can't reach the bustling frontroom anonymity he seeks so desperately, & who can blame him: a group of tattooed kagouled disruption fiends invade his party are threatening the scene juss by being here; scaring the shit outa whoever harbours thoughts they're not welcome at the party whoever's the bottle to throw a do in their city without inviting them in first place, coming down the hall towards me all eyeballs one third up stairs: conspicuously placed like kermit's nephew i find myself centrestage. leadman starts chat to me & me mate, sits close on stair to invade my space & from a drug induced inability to judge distances, his crew raising chins as they wait for an excuse to start battering the people & place

"alrigh boys"

   "whatchu on star?"

cardiff cut

but doan wait for reply

"i'm gonna sit by hhurr & you can talk to us"

meaning he was gonna talk ta me. i nod & start rolling, for diplomacy.

"you kairdiff? where ju live?"

i tells while he goes giving eyeball which i meet (avoiding could well spell the enda me, or at best a long wait in emergency), he decides to test me knowledge of local geography/the city grid

"so where you from/roath yeh? so wassis?"

"student party"

"uh?"

"cathays"

"so where's flora street? fanny street?"

"flora i ain't met mate, but there's fanny aplenty all over the place"

the biggest of his mates tries upping the pace witha

"gimme tha spliff"

aimed at me face but i keeps poker & tell im

"give me a fuckin chance mate. i'm gonna finish rolling, spark it up, have a smoke then pass it on to this friend of yours with whom i am fuckin talking, then if HE wants ta pass it on: you'll

be sorted"

which i reckons adds up to both paying dues & disrespect; leaves the cunt having to accept, unless he wants ta challenge rank withiz buddy (my mouth already open i realise too late/this nite makes me cocky)

harmless approaches & sez

"up yet gents?"

gobby fat 'gimme that' sez

"go fuck yaself"

"ok my friend; keep it calm; just being sociable/just asking on the off chance..."

(your endorphins beg to swim & dance...)

(a school of soaring unemployment dolphins cohabit with cutathrust sharks).

fatboy has the look of deciding but his topmate cuts in with iz lightning reaction/begins to laff at the *fanny* crack like it really deserved a response, convincing the oppressive twat to shut his mouth/he'll have to wait/to leave it out, goes looking for some other poor sod to get in his way. the other two follow unimpressed, convincing me i've the lucky touch enuf tonite to doublebluff me way thro this minefield of potential kickings *(you may cuff me roughly round the ears if you desire but it'll cost ya)* the biggest threat fell for it/went on his way, never in a million years/my getting away with a gobby turn is something they rarely accommodate *(the number of kickings i could've avoided jus by shutting my face...)*, so juss ride the wave with an inner smile & incredibly not one dysfluent break it seems

42

cardiff cut

i've convinced them if not meself/not one stammer to give
away...

the spanner sat beside me laffs & sez

*"you ever do H man? there are times when i find myself on
the streets of kathmandu... you ever been there star? when
the last i knew was well listen to me now... you should try it...
take my word"*

& puts his hand inniz pocket. i looks inniz eyes *(kathmandu?
this guy ain't even seen newport)*; tries to catch up with the
leap in time to follow this bloke's vision line to break the link
with a flintlite, inhale, exhale, figure his intake pass him the j &
smokesay

"nah mate, i'm alright"

he takes j off me hands, inhales & replies

"you sure about tha?"

& when i say

"yeh mate, the dot's doing fine"

he gess up/presses flesh & goes join his compadres: they have
a seat & a beer waiting too close to a group of young women
*(less juss hope they keep it in their pockets: can't have these
fuckers breeding)*. i finish me can on the stairs.

above: i'm aware of a peoplecrawl reinhabiting the staircase.
below: the crew in the hall re-emerge from carpet/wallpaper,
about face, look at me as if to say

"everything alright mate?"

but no one sez so i say nothing but look to me mate who looks down the hall to the boys in the kitchen & back to me & speaks thro his gaze but to everyone else we are pokerfaced the both of us jus getting on & saying nothing. he puts his hand in the carrier & we drink our own beer leave them to the free in the fridge: no point in taking the piss/pushing me luck to the limits, you never know i may need it/sooner than i think.

some prick under pressure from the relieved sense of danger comes accusing with his best expression of anger & gets onta me witha

   "are they YOUR fucking friends?"

in a perfect non accent looking to blame me/looking to reassert himself. no problems, i leave him with eyeball &

"they are now mate"

the all that's needed short stare of he who comes thro a manshit hurricane with the shine still there on his buttons (i am neither oppressor nor oppressed; i am enigmatic when challenged; i have succeeded where he didn't dare; my brain is in need of/completely aware & if i don't get a change of scene it could come crashing away/need to get offa these fuckin stairs i reckon...)

i flick up me head & me mate heads for bedrooms. i trail.

cardiff cut

spanish landing:

climb stairs; me mate sidles thro without spilling his beer & i almost mirror, having shouldered thro men i gently change shape/pull the torque of my shoulders when few steps remain i squeeze thro two women leantalk at the top of the case, gess eyeball from some sexy spanish superminx who won't let me pass til she sez with her hands & face

"hola"

i turn my head in the general direction & say

"iya"

but don't focus til feel her hands work me chest & downward, leans to me ear & digs in her accent

"hhhchnice body"

all seductive (i find it hard not to laff in her face/i knows no cunt's ever daft enuf to pretend i'm a beefcake; unfounded flattery to me implies fuckall respect; i'm shitfaced & could jus imagine this)

"did you say something?'

"yes i said: hhhchnice body. now what is your name?"

amazing. amusing. amazing cos i'm a streaka piss/more meat on a dog's bone/more fat on a chip/me only sixpack a placky fulla tins & amusing cos for fucksake i may be accounted for but i can still appreciate. she looks smells smoulders deadnice/the inviting darkcurl of the olive european. so i sez thro the nearest i can pull to a cheeky grin

"thanks very much"

(well what else can i say?) tell her me name & keep walking *(i may be out of but still devoted/ain't burning me bed/ain't blaming the acid...).*

i join mate sat on landing. he gets one together: we share; have a laff between ourselves/beware not to taint the rare status of audience when relaxed under threat & not only survive but able to say

       "who them?

             nah!

   iss cool man

       not a prob

they're safe"

of avoiding a battering without losing face & then getting feltup in bargain; inhale...

....

me mate goes check out the music downstairs: problee got his eye on some body. i gess meself as far as the next room/sit on the bed & sez to the smat of people juss kinda sat there

"anyone fancy a j?"

occasional faces lite up while others up & away. i return polite chat to those who remain

"blahblah, bunkbunk... "

cardiff cut

"hey what's your name friend?..."

they look to me, but talk to me joint.

i roll a few & talks to this girl who's sat next on the bed & fuck
am i spooned/have become somewhat angular: my brain
dumps/my speech corrupts disrupts erupts into ppppppppp
pppppurrrowlonngaisssshun & BBLOCK! which does her head
in. i explain my stammer is currently exacerbated by the use of
various substances but for her it is accurate & crisp
pronunciation or i shouldn't be allowed on the street; the
moment is lost for ever, the miracle of fluent speech has worn
off so for me its back to the gel&merge the mel&guh the
guhguhgerge/a more normal degree but who knows for how
long before i can spe who knows for how long befor i ca befo i
can glide communicatively, befor people stop thinkin *O leave
him he's pisst* remember freedom is only ever temporary. *so
what?* fuck fluency. i unwrap a microdot, go halfsies with a
bloke with an E, blag some speed. realise aristo's alsatian has
grafted itself onto the head sitting next to me: asks if i've a
twenty so she can tube up the powdery

"a twenty!? at this time a nite? you'll be fuckin lucky..."

me a stammering cheapskate she wasn gonna waste on me but
spanish siren turns facesaving saviour/walks into backroom
finds me close to another & encourages to remove her pale
english arse. nice touch. *southpaw* does as she's askt.

this señorita has flavour; gives orders to skin up so i accept
offer & use her gear. she chats & eyes, looks up from a line,
great brows over deepbrown eyes. i reply reserved yet
dynamic; mix up me message to give moment to breathe/to let
substance take place/to decide what's my scheme, desperately
tryna operate on two levels at once: stay straight yet get off it;

loyal yet flirtatious; take stock of the energies.

she's alright; a fine, vivacious, horny mediterranae about ten years younger, lets me know more when i asks more about her, inhales into lungs so deep she could burn the blow outa spliff without staining the roach/without torching the tip.

bassbins pump mattress/come thro beams to our cheeks. i'm fidgeting now cos a sober clash & i know i ain't gonna do anything tonite; the only transference of juice the spit on the roach; gonna smoke with her but nothing else; gonna soak up her vibe & enjoy the touch/the rub of brief thigh & personality brush but i've home to go back to/a woman in me life, so soakup but don't let her squeeze out the sponge.

we chat. i tell her what it's all about as in: straight with her, tells her she's nice but she ain't gonna get any from me tonite/i am accounted for, but if she wants ta share a while then dim problemo. so we smoke & chat. she don't give a monkey's i stammer; tells me of her exboyfriend back home in españa/a character who sat on their sofa taking gram after gram & weed after weed banging self high/banging erectile on green/tuggd himself floppy between six & eight hours continuously. daily. she had enough. or didn't as the case may be. & kickt him out. he claimed the weed made him want it but the speed stopt him climaxing/blamed it on her choice of channels which he sat up all nite watching. last heard he paid penance running naked round an isolate monastery on some ex leper colony island, beating himself mercilessly. *heesh.* almighty.

me mate comes back & suggests we move. we're getting ready out but she wants to come too, i say

"well it's up to you buh we're jus gonna go back watch some tube, you might wanna hang around, find yaself a lovspoon"

me dying to fuckyfuck but know where my priorities lie; why the choice fights the sense; knowing besides everything else i'd never get it up with a bellyload of beer draw & chem, but iss gonna take a while to get her out of my headbed

she stays/we go, but not befor a grab of me arse/befor sharing her mushrooms with me & me mate.

we leave/head downstairs only shrooms take immediate effect/go straight to me gut: needs a dump/dart upstairs.

there's a lovers' tiff taking place in the lav, i stands by the door & let my ears flap as one sez to other

   "but NO ONE will EVER love you like i do, you realise that."

not so much dedication as shoehorn & shotgun into zones of emotion control. i hear silence from the girl & her thoughts; kick at the door & threaten to *punch his fuckin lites out* if he don't make a move outa, but don't; just think about it for a moment. the door opens & their storm blows into hall, they consider their rôles but we're already downstairs & whatever woke in me gut i gotta get *out!* & pronto.

we endup in garden by mistake: i wass juss follow me mate but here we are so he sits on the grass & talks, i get in the cornershade & shit away/tellsim about spaniard/about potential, he sez

   "aren't you jus a little piqued?"

"not yet, but i'll say when i get there"

   "& where would that be?"

"as hi as the crashrate at coryton i reckon..."

realise after while there is pain; i am crouched on a nettle; my arse is in space/feels not hurt but intense, sensual; sensations shimmy up me arse & make me aware

me mate sez

    "woss up wi your face?"

decide to leave this place so pulls up & buckle, checks i'm still in one piece & load up me pockets, enter the house & consider exit strategies/our get away/our *"meet you at the gate"*. say

"tara "

to whoever stands close enuf & long enuf for me to articulate.

the girls from the store/in the kitchen grab &

    "ay, which way you goin?"

offer to walk us there.

cardiff cut

city road:

flyposters announcing

> *'late nite flava'*

(i see *phantasia*'s shut again)

a stagger of moonbeaters pass the 9-til-5's not fusst about
finding ways home/too busy filling face wi burgers, kebabs, &
kinell! a bag fulla donuts *(stay away from the hole).*

city road:

helicopters tracking video pirates & raving airwave buccaneers
careening careering stolen cars with stereo at maximum/
handbrake turns into

bedford street:

campervans wired up to the neons (free electric thro the nite, a
dodgy gas canister leaks on the quiet, come morning: a fifty-a-
day-man stops alongside, sparks up & takes half the street sky
hi. for a whole day it'll rain ikea & habitat: bedford refurnished,
sodium bright)

some kid leans & shouts outa upstairs window

> *"mayday! mayday!"*

mother screams from neighbour's bed

> *"get ta sleep ya little bastard or i'll take ya mobile away"*

up & inta tha next road not straight enuf to care/nearly knockt
over by a big red&blue: fucka nearly killed us; anyone'd think
there was a fire or sumit

"O; right; yeh"

we ain't quite withit today.

sign in the window of a zenbuddhist temple

'p/t staff required (apply within)'

("part time zen? sowasssaden?")

my knees go when we slow in the dark. so keep walking.

get back to the flat. the girls walk with us to frontdoor, one sez

"we'll come in fora cupa but we're goin home to bed"

"yeh, right, yeh..."

we go up a flight, make sarnies, a cupa & smoke; a table fulla teastains/lotsa little blimburns/empty bottles/full ashtrays/ discarded filters & roach. i take off me hat&coat, settle in to a comfy seat & remind meself of this cheeky little mexi. begin the first of many searchpatrols for the telly remote.

the girls stay a while. one writes down a number which she gives to me mate, have forgotten their names by the time they vacate (i ain't renowned for remembering, but they was good companions while we paralleled trips).

i watch telly with the vol down, plug home arcade into second set; go footy & rally while me mate hits the decks: too much like hard work in his present state so sticks on a tape.

we go over the nite; go over old stories from previous nites; get stoned watchin tv & video & playstat & watchin&makin & watchin&makin coming down & popping up buildin splifters & interruptions by *love me tender* coming up thro floorboards (*or have i juss made that up?*) mingled with the spice aroma from curryhouse below listenin to sounds smokin pure Trans Am grass flown fresh express from mate out honduras & mexico. giggle delivery outblasts the typical british sledgehammer badlymash vegetable matter mong of the brain of fact this grass the best gear since amsterdam days, for defo

(the dam:

cruising canals & vondel park getting thrillstoned on shared j's benches coffeeshops hotel bedrooms banks tourist information tramlines bus stops anywhere we could physically roll one running risk of six foot blondes on bicycles tried ta cross on zebras but so hot the paint melted didn't notice nearly killed us mowed down by trams as jellyboots got stuck on flytrap white line stripes of venus attracting the stoned didn't see the cones & the bloke in the overalls staring deadfurious as we giggled in his stillwet handiwork; clambering black tarmac in search for new surfaces where we could still walk; trundled ignoring traffic signs cars bus trams bikes stagger tryna grasp plastic from roadsweat path of trucks; breaking sandal straps & going nowhere nowhere fast going nowhere at all to be honest fuckin lafft in thirtyfive wholesome degrees; heading for museum & cool of bold paintings hung in halls in galleries but still stuck on globulous velcrofloor dancing & sniggering to the sound of carhorns singing

"fucking british tourists look where you're going!"

we were unable to answer coherently so aided our feet as best we could manage, found a mister minit still giggling & pay tha man strut the shop with shoes done up & continued j-walking to the museums & those grass enhanced fabulous van gogh paintings, leaving twirls of white footprints as a a thanks for the memory...

but that whole amsterdam trip was gonna be weird from the very first minute: waiting for the coach on a cold summer morning coming down from the nite before, popping over the road to download me intestines last chance til aust services/better out; using the spacey fucking toilet on wood street: i was having a smoke on the lav & jus tryna chill meself down when the cubicle flusht itself out, i'm sitting on a comedown wi me feet in the air tryna keep it together while below there's redafuckindair spraying pinefresh floorclean over me jeans & trains; piped music over top of this i couldn't be certain if it was really there like there for real, walks out the slideydoor like i'm in *the tomorrow people* unsure if i'd find the world normal or as close as it was when i left to go in, fuckin toilet did me head in, stay away mate i warn ya, felt like *mister benn* & *mister bean* all rolld together for the rest of the day...)

(remembers the nite i was so off me face at victor drago's in falmouth: new year's eve & final nite befor bulldozed; laffing so much i shat on the dancefloor people still dancing *did i tell you that?* now i know i'm arseholed/there's a little secret i ain't screamingly proud of...)

story stories anything to laff; video & playstat; rolling up; putting budbites into little bags & proclaiming

"weed's for smoking in bed man"

> *"yeh right!*
> *you get this lovely warm high getsya just right for some*
> *loving"*

"i was thinking more like: there ain't no hotrocks burning holes thro the duvet"

> *"yeh man, that's right, jus what i'm saying"*

(some confusion between animals & their domesticated living).

....

startin to nod. the girls i remember have already fuckt off.

(chugchugchugchugchugchugchug...)

the telly in corner throws random visuals at pace with our

overenthusiastic use of the remote controller; we flick on a special news broadcast &

"ang on a mo/turn it up a sec"

"we interrupt your late nite viewing to go straight to the steps of city hall…"

(whitehaired oldgoat in a bigman suit standing on the steps being interviewed, microphones & keylites all aimed at him, looking shagged out yet still smooth as he announces…)

"i appreciate all the commotion i'm causing, but i'd like to assure you as befits my status as city mayor: (pause for breath) i've fuckt enough tarts in this job to feel disgusted with them & enough pleasant girls & boys to feel disgusted with myself, what more can i say? nothing's been so great as the opportunity you the populous have afforded me in allowing me to fuck your metropolis both ways, oh & while i'm here: you were great!"

"…i'd also like to reassure the public the voters my colleagues & political allies my family & friends my wife the wives of my friends of my colleagues the public voters & my political allies: i DID get my money's worth; she'll never walk again."

(from the press:)

"sir! isn't this the straw to break the camel's back?"

"i don't think her parents will appreciate you calling her a camel, youngman."

"mr mayor, how do you see yourself getting out of this? who is your own worst enemy sir? is it yourself?"

"i'd prefer not to inform them of their status."

"but sir, where does the city go from here?"
        ("surely you can't deny us, a reply at least!?")

"well listen here, this is the the boss man ruling & i recommend you do whatcha dig & dig whatcha do & then all ya dig & all ya do live up to the name teenager - tommy steele, 1958, i remember it like yesterday, as advice goes: it's diamond."

(an aside from an aide:)

"sir best not go into that now/sir, you're rambling/advise you to shut/up at once..."

(but having a taste for the mic carries on:)

'...but i still have something to do to this city/ something to say/to repay to this city & the city has a debt to pay me..."

(the squeal of microphones being dragged by their leads)

"...so my advice to you, members of the public gentlemen of the press, is: be wary of shiestas & charlatans, shamsters merchants policymakers grant applicators masturbators self-proclaimers amateurs & big mouths: pocketliners one & all. you heard it here first, trust none of them, & a good nite for now."

(from one young journo who can't take no:)

"but sir! but sir! isn't it true you're just a mad old loon?"

"laddo, i'll leave you with something my old nan used to say: my history's long me dick is short i'll see you fucking cunts in court *now thank you & good nite. any more questions direct them towards my brief."*

"(constable, bring me that bastard immediately, he'll do for the home trip...)"

"that's right son: an exclusive interview; better come with me..."

(he's led off to the mayor's blackwindowed van, flanked by chemicalsuited government men)

(a wheezy old fullashit hack coughs up:)

"where will you go mayor?"

"i expect to be back in my office conducting my duties by the end of next week. until then i'll be spending my suspension i mean vacation *away from the nation/unavailable to my friends in the press: orders of the court & out of respect for the dead. but i'll be staying at my holiday home in..."*

(synchro city:
    where the loudest people are those outraged by unsolved sexcrimes/the rape of a young child/the splitting open of a girlfriend's smile not cos of offence towards their religious rights humane instincts or belief in a sense of moral justice but cos they can't abide the thought of someone else getting away with what keeps them up all nite in their own sexual frenzy/over such acts as they can only dream about/such bestial fantasies only available to those of the most righteous house)

(& cut to the studio:)

"well CALIGULA'S HORSE! CAESAR'S WIFE! there you have it: the mayor of this fine city operating like a door to door salesman out of a sexual suitcase..."

(behind the anchorman a screen shows the mayor scream from the back of a speedin van/a ford *jury* if i'm not mistaken:

"the birds are blue! i am the truth! i am the truth!")

"...alias victor de bastos, hilcrois mainch, AKA joyo macphfister, otherwise known as hoopla van drago or vinus le plate but more recently: simply MISTER MAYOR to one & all"

"...& now: a short break".

me mate sez nothing. can't be sure he heard it even. all i know is aristo's gone barking if he thinks i'll get a shot off from here.

(late nite telly livened up for once, followed by an ad from the sleep council telling us to kick the evening into touch. flick to the news on another channel:)

"...i'm now going to pick up the receiver & speak live & direct not only to you the nation but also to city hall:"

"hello?"

"hello?"

"hello?"

"hello, is this the county of cardiff policy unit?"

"maybe. do you want the policy unit or the policy policy unit?"

"uh, well young lady i'm not sure..."

"then i cannot assist you"

"miss, this is a special news broadcast..."

(click, burrgh)

(1001 questions to ask of your city, i'm sure.*)*

"to all our viewers at home: i'm sorry to say this was a realtime interchange with a city official..."

"now to bob on the steps of the national museum: bob, please tells us, what IS going on?..."

(the last act of the mayor was to drive the remaining newscrews spare, with tears streaming down their cheeks they're captured live on screen, ever reliable bob for example:)

"please mama! not the cupboard! she shat in the cupboard! she shat in the cupboard! my cupboard! that's my cupboard mama! only i'm allowed to shit in there get outa my cupboard mama come on get out! of my cupboard come on ma it's my turn now..."

(so back to the studio:)

"uh we seem to be having a problem... bob can you hear us you ARE on air..."

"...& take ya filthy shit droppings with ya... hey andreas is that you? this is bob at the museum: made it ma, i'm top of the world!"

(andreas kicks over camera five as he's carted away from the studio, within a week he'll be back on sports, *let's praise the lord...* andreas: a secondrate suit who wears it badly; a non-accent taff who takes it up the valleys; the ultimate weird as he's know in the industry cos he's just too fuckin normal & his nose too shiny; he's spent thirty years in a smoking lounge hanging on the end of a coloured sobranie waiting for that call/waiting to get outa harlech but it never came, *poor bastard...*)

(this from a floorhand in cans, leans over the newsdesk &:)

"*now over to our* international america *correspondent* spoony jim *with this report from mosscowww...*"

"*jeezus andreas what's going on there!? we've just got news from a satellite station on the mongolian plains that the lord mayor of wales laid the gross national income put the lot on a bet on a shortsighted horse called* yes yes gabalfa, *broke a leg in the 2.30 at chepstow. can you clarify? what were the odds? did it finish the race? how many runners?*"

"*well jim, money goes where money knows, let's just say the funds have left wales*"

"*so does this mean ANOTHER referendum?*"

the mayor last seen driven down to the mudflats, a rubber dingy outa the barrage & away from the delta, flashcode directions to catcha sub off the bay & away downriver. splitsecond timing before barrage sealed in (he had a map of the sunken structures). never seen again: the mayor, the sub, the mudflats under a pisspot marina where it's unhealthy even for fish to swim.

once onboard the mayor sends a wire a pulse a satellite

broadcast to okayama, niigata, weimar, sömmerda, mount olympos cyprus, asturias, earth station goonhilly, parkes observatory new south wales, plymouth's wilderness road & home sweet home terrace, glynmercher isaf, west 12th street new york city, madley british telecom, jodrell bank, ely fields, out to the planets; checks coast & downs periscope, dragging a local fishing boat to a watery grave, drugging himself up from sleep, he *who walkedst the foaming deep*, & below the waves.

(a spokesman sez:)

   "to the city of my birth i speak for our mayor, bouncing off of satellites he wishes to share his reasoning with you: put simply: charm is a con. remember this is true"

(the mayor in the background:)

      "uncle ho! uncle joe! i'll sue for peace! i'll sue for war! i suggest you amend your profit & loss/my vote's in the post/i'll sell wales offshore/glug glug/(laugh to close)"

(back to the frontman:)

      "he no longer remembers being your mayor".

the police meanwhile are tryna focus their global positioning system to locate the mayor to within an eighth of an inch; track down his DNA to various sites across the grid & find him still with us up the arse of the welsh office, county of cardiff & WDA (consider phoning meself, to track down the telly remote absorbed somewhere inexplicable between settee & fridge).

(broadcaster:)

   "well, that's it for this very special broadcast, we'll bring you updates as news comes in, we'll always be the first to

break, but for now remember: you arseless cunt... i'm sorry that's a correction: you arseholes COUNT"

("can we go to a break? it's been a helluva nite, crack open the champagne...")

(powerbrass & drum to fade...).

reflectin on the window is: bluelite. i gess up, takes a look. outside there are two police cars spinning beneath me, a third does a handbrake turn/takes off down alley

"wad tha fuck is..."

i gess paranoid quite easy. tryna figure out where to hide the gear. crouch behind curtains to get a clear view & i can see em in the carpark so they ain't coming here (*but why down the lane? to keep the fire escape covered it gotta be... jeezus christ they're gonna come in from both directions... it must be the fish... the fish the grass was in...*)

i hear clumping above me. have a go at the ceiling. reckon police in the alley musta parktup by now must be almost in by now consider grabbing baseball bat & catching the fuckers half thro backwindow. thought about, but not my cupa at the best to be honest. allow meself a moment's doubt/consider the longshot: jussa bad case a willies bringing me down like an acme elevator manned by wile e. coyote (or should that read *dogged...)*

look out the front/follow raised voices. i see a cuffed boy being led away & in background a copper tryna climb a JCB (*chugchugchugchugchugchugchugchugchugchugchug chug... how long's that been in me ear?)* i watch em leave. go make a cupa tea. roll one while i wait for the sake of me head, watch a bit more telly (doan know what me mate thinks but it's fuckall ta do wi me).

....

discussion ona box over who will pay the vast majority of legal costs for chasing the mayor over missing funds over the rest of europe over interpol's insistence on the existence of offshore bank accounts & getting in contact with our man in the caymans, our cow on the channel isles, our missile in cuba. this between the government & a senior councillor:

"we will pay the vast majority."

"sure you will, but how large a majority?"

"the very most."

"how much exactly?"

"let's not get bogged down in accounts... but i'd say forty percent tops."

"but that's NOT the vast majority!"

"according to my figures it is the lion's share of projected costs barring unforeseens of course which should get mopped by a slush i mean crush i mean crash option on repatriation of reclaimed balances from this man's crimes"

"but forty percent is not more than half!"

"it's my accent isn't it? if you're going to make it personal this discussion is over. good night."

by now mister mayor must've sat with the captain, dined on the best, four course & cocktails (an aristo speciality, the chef having mysteriously choked to death: until then no one realised there were donuts in the galley, the captain forced to pressgang a caterer in cardiff, aristo ideal: heard mentioning his days in the navy, tho more like an arms run on the rosslare ferry).

tomorrow my negs will show handshakes of thanks in the galley. no one looking more pleased than aristo, no one more gullible than the mayor & the captain (aristo's been deepcover for over twenty years, shuffling cheap espionage of fantasy & fear & building files stored in his wisdom teeth: a one man sexcrime secret police; a stasi of videograb; a politburo of deceit, tracking money transfers across the inward investment economy. now he's all the proof he needs it's time to leave. i'll get my cheque around tuesdee, & a compliment slip...)

(*aristo?* he was there at the smoke riots when the mayor announced blanket bans in public places; there when the mayor began barcoding babies; there behind the two-way mirror when ambassadors practised the anthem; there at the authorisation of funds to be spent on refurbishing the apartment; there in the tunnel leading from welsh office/leading comfort women to the bunker below hodge building... the city pound they talked of was their stash of little women, some as old as their teens, some not even female. *O aristo: now where do i go for me beer money?*)

....

put a little pack in me pocket & prepare to leave for home (when ya mates are all tuned to channel nine you know it's time to get off the line, i no longer know how to be). roll one for the road, put on me coat, wave to me mate, retire from the scene. walk out the room & immediately back in, pick up me hat & some skins. me mate's already asleep; will wake up at teatime still sat on settee. switch off the telly & leave.

once down the dark tunnel of stairs it is: pale blue sky; sunnyday for those just waking; feels like dawn but i know it's much later; earlymorn lite & the moon is collapsing

me? i reckon a kip'll do me.

cardiff cut

city road:

negotiate speedfreak with his three rottbull crossbreeds *maxwell murdoch berlusconi* stomping the street like a mayday parade; three snouts tear muzzles, the only ones here are me & them. stop by a newsagent for sweets: still shut; early edition bundles scream

       'hubba bubba gone deep'

           referring to the mayor's longterm moniker based on his early career remit of bursting pinko bubbles with his political teeth (first emerged on frontpage with *'hubba bubba killed clubba'* but this contemporaneous reporting/never made second print, his legalteam saw to this. the evidence lost once taken from scene, the clubba carbondated then buried ina tobacco tin. never did find his identity; never did rest in peace).

newport road:

gotta get home/try upping me speed, first i gotta cross this six laned street

(rear red glow/undersill indigo/headlites shine lilac; futuristic vehicles hover eastbound carriageway, leave tracers of transit...)

       central reservation

    (shadows of infirmary; whiteclouds buzz smudge of blurred buildings in fronta me...)

          kerb & pavement.

takes a piss in a shagbattered doorway, aware of it cold but no feel it juss steam. the old lloyd's bank sprayed

'jacks' & 'scfc'

tho long painted out can still read it beneath (cheekybastards, if you looks close enuf it becomes unremitting/at this time of morning: a smack in the teeth)

& i'm stopping&starting & stopping&starting like the stations of the fuckin cross *(i thought you wuz ina rush?/get home ya daft cunt...)*

....

cardiff morning seagulls make me think everytime of working wi me uncle geoff/working on the vans: early starts to RAF lyneham after nites of skittle lock-in's at labour clubs around the city; rows of brass coloured handles reflecting suggestions of sun down canada road at four in the morning; a gastric of gulls chanting us outa town & up sixty foot scaffolding, hoovering asbestos dust & carrying fullbags down welldodgy ladders, loading vans & chopsing...

remember once took a fag break at lyneham & called into next hanger for toilet, got told by a gasmask to

"get the fuck out!"

SLR to me stomach (taceval state: bikini red)

"why's that?"

"out of bounds; been blown up"

(of course it has, does your wargame allow me to piss in the hedge?)

(alert state still at black alpha).

next day fellow worker about same age goes missing, presumed bogbound & skiving/sly ciggy & crossword. MPs inform foreman the kid's been arrested, ran up controltower screaming

"the germans are coming!"

took four to get him back out (what freaked em was how he passt patrols on special alert, small arms cockt against backa van mortar attacks/not expecting freakouts from hired hands in paintsplat overalls while ultravigilant of the outside world).

pisst ourselves on way back ta city tho never seen again. if i remembers he was instituted. christ knows what he's doing now... problee find him down at rhoose airport in charge of airtraffic.

newport road:

white sierra pulls up to sell me some weed. check iss no secondrate DS entrapment scheme; checks to see it's not those two pseudo rastas who kidnapped me in interest of market stability (wouldn't let me out their sierra til i bought up their stash of cack henna, diesel & chewing gum gear: tasted shit & did nothing); checks ta see it's not those white geezers followed me & me partner walking up elm street: did a hand brake turn outside yellow kangaroo parkt across pavement & watched & waited for us to gain (we were heading city road thro shelley gardens decides instead to walk newport road wordsworth avenue down lane, no point walking into a setup when you're aware of the scene), did me head in, the bastards were grinning from ear to ear (when pickin out the headfucks nature precision scans the cultures of the city, sticks every single nutta in a secondhand sierra & sends em out witha dash fulla fotos of me)

but no problem: these guys wuz jus buzzin, show em me spliff to show not in need, *take it easy*

(gotta get on; avoid potentially hazardous asteroids on me way home).

....

on my right: home of the infamous cardiff-greek computer geek

'gates inconstantuse'

(bloodybig sign for all to see).

chat heard four elms by bog behind library

"waylon nicked that cash wyn"

"who waylon did?"

"got blamed for it"

"yeh well doan go grassin: it was me... & doan go tellin waylon neither, i'll figure something meself see...".

great smell coming out of the meghna balti tandoori takeaway tho closed (used to get extra food from there cos the bloke had a thing for me missus. she thought. so i always said for her to go fetch it. great food, fair-do's no really great food, & she'd come home with extra portions. shame she won't go no more;

70

refuses).

....

on corner of four:

taxi stops at lites (*didn't i blow your mind this time* - the delphonics); moves off befor i gess sight of the drive

- - - - - - - - - - - *voorrrr*

upper clifton street:

the pizza kitchen (celebrity patronage); golden house (finest cantonese cuisine, best chinese takeaway this side of river/best chinese takeaway & jus round the corner givin big portions free crackers nice welcome for us we are regular customers, every year a calendar, every week a meal); levant kebab shop (queue up & play the arcade machine, *gimme everything & chips, can't you see i'm pisst & hungry?*)

broadway:

snooker hall; la, la, zar halal (recommended by me uncle john); superstar fish bar tandoori & balti (still open at four in the morning, free delivery anywhere in cardiff but it seems i always walk)

clifton street:

tony's la gondola (great roast & brecky restaurant; absolute top spot); lucky star chinese; newly opened café sheeva; boa vista portuguese (just a sitdown place, announcing new management every other week, i hear it tastes tho i've never been); royal bengal tandoori (once a personal favourite - proximity privacy cheap, an empty table never a problem, good for a little love escape or after pub feast); clark's sitdown & chippy (been using the *pop-in diner* on&off since a kid); the *clifton* & *tred* either end of the street.

pisst old scroat ofa bloke shouts to me

  "alright chief!"

waving his carkeys, wears a badged blue blazer & a carrier full of empties. thinks he lives in a car in me street

i hear *laffingman* echo...

& *heptan jeremy* was follow me. couldn't quite catch he hidden in doorways alleys in the amberlite shine offa windscreens. big fat lean lanky squat streaka piss obese beard cleanshaven specs coloured contact lenses twentytwenty vision i couldn't see him but he could see me. kinda guy. i find it hard ta trust him myself find someone him the same as i. sneaking around thro the fucking nite weird you ask me... i can sense him thro adamsdown thro this diamond mine between splottrack & newporoad where we bomb out the policestat & bejewel our roads with sapphire street emerald street ruby & topaz, diamond street pearl street agate *(house of bingo)*

nora helen cecil bertram terraced to beresford road

gold street silver street platinum, copper street lead zinc tin & iron, metal street where me father schooled, st. german's church, orbit street planet street comet eclipse & moon, system street sun & star, constellation & meteor

augusta moira leopold anderson galston garesfield clyde & kames, adamsdown square, adamsdown lane. footbridge & railtrack, cemetery park & student flats, cardiff prison over the way, north & south luton place

cardiff cut

longcross street & infirmary, four elms road & piercefield place

stacey road priest road, elm partridge oakfield, fox booker fort.
roath. whitewashed funeralhome on newport road, the royal
oak, into place

    territory

unfolds

& home to sleep. or at least to eat. fuckin starving me.

phonebox outside policestat:

couple in there having a bit, heard they do it regular/every opportunity/any event/wherever they can get their coin in the slot/whenever they can hear the pips run out.

sapphire street:

proposed site of streetlite marked in yellow paint

'SoL'

(the *'o'* shows the base of the column/where it will enter the public slab/already vibrates whitefinger); sense of reassurance seeing trees grow thro turning bay/turning circle/bubbling the tarmac

& outside the postoff on clifton street the belisha's stuckup ta glory from hands from prams/fulla halfeaten sweets, the sweat offa protest stickers, pensioners, dolees, the fear of people tryna cross between a thousand daily sandwich stops who gotta get back quick *fuck those on their feet they can wait we're busy.*

charity shop on same side of street sells viscount tonypandy's suits (tailored or not they still don't fit tho i did buy a blacktie on me way to a funeral) & the shoebox markt *'literature'* bare but for mills&boon, studynotes & the occasional political memoir.

copper street:

'bomb rhiwbina'

cardiff cut

a deserted television (bare wire showing, plug pliered off), hooch bottles smashtup to the mosque. in background: the flying buttressed st. german's church, echoes from *king of the nippers* heard...

as i cross to ruby some ragtag pussycat straight outa the neighbourhood (*spot from splott* possibly) gives a dirty look.

ruby street/curry street:

'queer'

(sprayed on sidewall of woolies)

outside 2^5 is inexplicably written

'i don't love you'

not even

'anymore'

to align with context;

to define the loss.

✦

reach house: yale mail check postmarks writing senders' addresses: postcard from sal states

'ALIEN INVASION'

timed to arrive with getting back from me trip (little injoke ongoing), the rest difficult to tell but there must be a cheque from aristo, he knows i've earned it.

stumble to settee, telly; presume sleep. remember i'm home so remove me hat&coat & try to chillout, ready to be woken by the early morn suffering shift of mushrooms beer & curry/bumbling down hall to the coolest seat.

stare at the telly. get up & turn on. *the learning zone* or fifty channels of talking shit even cartoons above me this morning even *sesame street*. try & hang in but the portable aerial keeps throbbing keeps calling me the co-ax cable snakes to back of set image jumps between red & green keeps flickerbeam tubeleap to eyes. screen disease. the blue blown outa this trinitron way back in the 70's.

fine for a while but now does me head in. can't be arsed to deal with this, down a coupla nurofen, wash down with the ouzo still where i left it miles ago hours ago at the start of the evening. a soak in the tub wash salt from me skin feel i've acquired a layer too many; of aching.

get up. run bath. check on sal; pop me head round bedroom door & world map falls from blutak on wall still tryna keep hold drapes to the bed but still she's not woken on her head falls the indian ocean & lands. creep in pull from & fold up (the least i could do). kiss lips cheeks & forehead: she doesn't stir *(sleep thro an atom bomb this one)*

cardiff cut

(i may call you: wonderful
you may call me: close to you)

my (bubble) of luv i wanna cuurrvvvvvvvWWWe
with her/nudge/ but leave, she sleeps on.

raid fridge. make a cupa coupla sarnies grab a packet of crisps
see what else there is, the ease with which a fresh yesdee
cream cake comes off the shelf & into me face has me
sniggering (cream busting thro lips).

cat wants feeding. pull a half can a felix rip red resealable
plastic lid & i swear to god the contents are moving but figure it
must be in me head cos when i fill his bowl & place on floor he
wolfs it/makes me think of potential for sick. a brandy. drop in
some icecubes & take a sip *(a sip? what am i saying)* stick all on
a tray & shift to the bathroom, go back switch off telly grab
bowl of many colours (bits & rizlas baccy lighters draw roach &
match, *'glassbottle/bottle glass'* - sense of humour if nothing
else) pour bubbles & prepare to get in. test the temperature.
my fingers don't taste too pink.

put a plank across tub & food up: plate of sarnies (fishpaste &
tom) crisps banana bourbons figrolls muga tea carton of o/j
bottla brandy glass with ice *(not like me: it seems i have an
empty leg tonite)* ashtray portable & tapes notepad pencilcase
coupla books whatever else seems necessary better take a shit
incase better pour another brandy.

sit on lav take a drag & move lock stock & bad stomach arse
cracks open & it's tearing me gut out ripping me arsehole
knarling snarling chomping at the bit i'm just waiting for it to
start talking (mushrooms take anal effect; follow thro every
moment).

so here am i, dumping a big greasyfood blackbeer fuelled lizard out me arse & you're telling me *it'll be alright/it serves you right* well thanks a fucking bunch pal (i converse with me rectum).

finish & flush. pick a coupla comics & move to the tub. seems good thro steam: bath run & ready to go. moist walls: one foot over realise i have yet to strip off my fingers slam & melt into them. slip off me stripey daps & work upwards. empty me pockets unload & take off & *my prize for the nite?* a grab of other people's lighters a phone number (no name) a match sleeve on which a strange hand has written

'GO FOR IT!'

in capitals, so even this meant for someone else.

take off specs & splash under cold, put in plug. compare myself; when i try to remember how i lookt earlier at aristo's when i lookt in the mirror what i see now a reflecting memoir i appear like me face in the chrome of a tap. plunge face down to porcelain crown of ice water, eradicate from within my brain the thirteenth bengal lancers dancing an equine mashup mashup coltrane quatrain sliding like a mental intestine burrowing burroughing scudfucking firespitting seasnake. burst from sink dismissing time as not yet spent & continue thro to windowsill blackgrime running down walls down grouting down eyes. steam on mirror i confuse with a wet hand. extremite matter bulldoze & placates i put on music me specs & climb towards bath.

the ache of the tub as i enter. *making music* by zakir hussain & if i remember a little bit of chopin tagged on the end. scratch one more turn from me own remaining lighter *(don't know what happened to the others i bought earlier)* spark up & tune in.

cardiff cut

....

lying ina bath witha wooden shelf across desperately tryna read tryna focus meself on *what is this?* miller's *tropic* or a *marvel* comic blowin spliff ash from page to page drinking deadman's brandy rolling hot & cold memories of ice to get ashtray; stub out *(where's me baccy?)* try to read & fail miserably, drink my tea & eat some food.

limescale & drywhite congeal of powdered milk whirls the surface/threatens to stir up the dregs of my intake/circulates radioactive falsetan sludge goo crud gulch mud in a cup more rings than a giant redwood. burnbristle tongue keeps taste at bay. i gulp without fear but i can sense it lactating, separating (the secretion of milk)...

(mr. shifter shitting t-bags out his arse on a box of PG; the coloneers of east anglia synchrotwirl their tartan flasks prodding me with

> *"drink up!*
> *it should be well stewed by now! "*

prod laybys with mugdrips & sandwich crusts

> *i should be home by now*

instead hassled by dualcarriage lunchbreaks while i'm hitchin along/away from these bastards if someone would stop

> *"we'd give you a lift ourselves but we're just having lunch...*
> *sandwich? no, we thought as much..."*

sudden surround of the blueflash of an accident tryna hitch home...)

...zzzzooooooooooommmm

gota get back to some here & now...

gota get back to the present zone...

gota zoom back to the bath & polish off; eat what i can.

soaking & (writing) & soakin & (writing) but all i come up with are one word monologues of minor existence *(ooo, ugg, shit, fuck, blimey)*.

remove stuff from shelf & shelf from bath balance ashtray between shampoos & edge of wet altar. steamy spliff to mouth. corner riz to hand spark & *fuckit!* dropt in bath

> *(ah... calm spliff in bath*
> *smoke & tubsteam relax... plop!*
> *kinell: spliff in bath...)*

start again. stick the wet to oneside (i'll put it in airing cupboard to dry with the rest... cackhanded excuse fora yak, not fit to run a bath, due to the demands on my attention span imposed by substances i feel devoid of ideas & incapable of controlling my hands... *fuck knows which orifice that came out of*).

....

smakt.

cooling towers on windowframe. reflections from litesource caught in foam bubbles, on bottles & bust tiles. other bubbles signify what ever crawled up me arse has decided to die there.

look at me water-distort body. bruises over shins & arms. it seems i've been bumping the world/at odds. plumprune toes blacknailed & penlegged with vigorous hair, bath oils reverberate, pluckt & played fuckt & maimed bathed greytile & pineclad steam air thickening knees penis bollocks more hair.

my specs steam up i remove them. don't seem much different. like the crumbs of me sarnie i disintegrate to bath/go under/

get distant.

slide down. my knees & nose islands. air leaves ears/bubbles up skin/pulses outskirt of shadow/takes tracers to surface. the displaced glugecho of water down overflow replaces it. *(tear offa strip! bomb the barrage! a puddle of glum/a secondhand mirage/tidal waves over cutknife cardiff!...)* lungs lift my cage. i turn my head to release the breath caught within orifices to fill with wet to cleanse the brain so i can sleep/drip amphet away.

so here is now. i steamwrinkle under levels above me/i am underground/am under necessity/have tunnelled to emerge into energy encased in hot water scumcovered the brown rings of the bath matching those of me teastained mug. raise a hand to the flannel & wipe, find lighter & smoke; pull a half j from ashtray & squeeze into lung space; try & slow the pace the weirdspace last steps before total comedown; suck the taproot of bluff.

....

the tape runs out. out there. i did nothing its STOP hum continues to round the room thro depths to fade. hear only the motor of my blood bounce the tub the water the brain the generation of ideas i cannot act on let alone recommend.

nothing like a steaming bath ina quiet room quiet cept for boiler churn producing plenty to top up true but listen: the water tank settles, the seagulls move on, the train sirens silent now the daylite's upon

at times silence the most noise of all

tune with my toes the tap not turned enuf to drum/not pummelling juss topping up/loop on fluid bass noise that slow consistent thud of hot water. tank whistle jazz. splash cymbals

cardiff cut

& beat of man O yeh it starts to kick off again.

instant little twists of hotrock wisp sonarblips to ears alongside rumble of tub. the presume pain of divebombs, flinchtwisting intensity of lava as i try further under but it's not really going on, hits but the relaxant of realisation: hotrocks cool in bathwater; red meteors cease & dark by the time they hit stomach are cooled of desire to burn. calm. trust the sound of my shallow lungs the pulse of my open heart speeding up to the slowing down close my inner eyes for now

pyroclastic flow to the coast

> *'truth is molten'.*

....

seed dreams:

ofa spirit ghost visit me & make a noise to freak me out/too/to open. turn head to scan but keep em shut turn side of bath to eyes then feel gentle rub ruffling smooth my hair against the tub reassuring as if attention seeking as if saying *try your vision/it's ok to wake*

dreamt last nite i climba hi-rise staircase, followed & pusht & plunged to the liftcage: infernal details escape but not memory of the man who pushed as i stood, turned, recognised the face the grin & the gabardine *(aristo? the mayor?)*

....

so could peerless jim be the greenstar shining brunel bright above us?

could an innocent bouncing queen street park place implode &

blow dylan's bar away? (an accident; volcanic redbrick ashtray; a gutted listed building)

could the duppy spirit of lynette white be the red dragon livery on cardiff's housing cheques uniforms & rubbish trucks? (scrubbed out in favour ofa crest of arms/city logo/a cymraeg motto/their fourth design in eight years)

so could cardiff be policed for the capture of rapist & woman killer, not *pin it on someone* but *of the guilty?* (lynette, lily volpert, geraldine palk... big investigations but solved they were not...)

....

consider a wank but can't get it up. fuckin comedowns.

cardiff cut

wake.

didn't know i was asleep.

blind by no shade/litebulb & sunlite bursting my face. take a while to retune to blue purple grey corpuscle floatings; for now juss enjoy this **wha wha** on view, my breath like a stick on railingssszzz

....

ceilingfloat & watch self in sleepmode. zoom back to bath & waking & open & suckt to the drumhum of four foot wingspan giant dragonfly waiting in top pocket of room. bandit at ten o'clock revving VAVOOOMMMM down from ceiling & just about to hit my face just about ta screw itself its sting to mouth & pulling back & ZOOMING back tryna focus tune into wiremesh of compound eyes & BOOF! & waking. the obvious *phew* checking the room *you just dream man iss cool* checking the room & smiling up to ceiling sunlite blasting checking the room & realising in the ten o'clock cover we are not alone. things happen faster now ZOOM! its coming down its gonna go right thro me skull any second now its gonna be fistfucking every facial cavity & BOOF! right thro me skull & BOOF! i wake up & *phew*. for real this time: dragonfly sunlite BOOF! wake dragonfly sunlite BOOF! wake *phew* dragonfly sunlite wake *phew* ZOOM *pleeease i fucking hate dragonflies* for real this time BOOF wake *phew* ZOOM BOOF *phew* ZOOM BOOF *phew* BOOF *phew* BOOF *phew* BOOF FUCKING BOOF BOOF *phew* ZOOM *fuckin phew* ZOOM BOOF ZOOM BOOF ZOOM BOOF *phew* coming round again *phew* bubble bubble *phew* *(is there no escaping this?)*

(dragonfly sunlite *phew* ZOOM BOOF *phew* ZOOM BOOF

phew ZOOM BOOF *fphew* BOOF *phhheuw* ZOOM BOOF
FUCKING BOOF ZOOM *phew* fucking *no i do not need this*
ZOOM *phew* ZOOM *phew* & thrashing thrashing & coffing my
fuckin heart up...)

   "he's coming round..."

                    thinkin: *this is madness iz madness...*

(flashback to newent crashlandin...)

   ....

i think it's been an hour now. since i've moved my head. under
insectile curfew trying not to see a thing to take the risk nor
sense movement in corners of ceiling try not to hear the
approach of sirens try not to think blink or provide a target nor
zoom tracers trace zoomers anymore than i have to.

tense.

(first time i experienced this: alexander road, plymouth; it took
me hours to leave me quilt let alone the room, nasty dose of
paranoia kept my movements few, & still do, i lie for hours.)

flanged.

burst to air

waking myself & half the street; remember why a sense of fate
to end a dream i must escape; scream the fucking house down;
evade the inevitable closing scene

accident?
   (acidnet)

cardiff cut

no safety net
    (to chance with)

the laws of chance
    (my screams were silent).

....

wake with a barking dog (this here's the catlands; we are not
bark tolerant for long) from shallow sleep on speed & acid; the
world comes awake & i cannot avoid witnessing won't hang
around too long can't see me making too much of it/the day
comes strong.

cat comes in & polishes off remains of paste sandwich. i take a
spot of brandy, smoke & try fathom what's going on, calm
down/come down but always listening, hearing, sliding round.

....

police helicopter beambusts on broadway; trains siren (both
asleep & awake) track noise thro water: drivers dicing with
toxic derailments under splottbridge & blazing stolen cars on
track; dragging waste down from north cardiff atomic weapons
establishment & to multinat pharmo biotech sites: labproduced
intermediate-level radioactive organic liquid waste; isotopes of
hydrogen used to trace the action of materials in the body cells
(reportedly cancer & heart disease) rated as

   'relatively harmless'

but when it enters the body & is organically bound research
claims it

   'dangerous'.

licences issued by the nuclear installations inspectorate state

'authorised by the environment agency to emit tritium & carbon 14 into the air & the sewer from its plant'

(tritium: naturally occurring radioactive substance given off by granite; released straight to air from fifty yard cooling towers; its liquid form, tritiated water; released to sewers lead to bristol channel... the fish within limits but not the anglers)

'world leaders in molecular research'

according to aristo's inhouse experts.

....

planes overhead. cardiff on flightpath of aircraft carrying materials for nuclear warheads from britain to the states *(surely the other way?)* which reminds: i still gota dig out the anderson shelter before i can contemplate growing any thing here in our buildingsite garden (alongside the shelter a longprevious occupant grew random brick structures the basis for walls, according to the neighbours for no reason at all. *bastard...*).

best known little known i shake myself in sleep; yagged shagged & stereotyped i sustain my recovery position til the cold water wakes me (feel pins&needles then the next sharp *ping!* realise water now freezing)

& sudden there's half the council workforce in me street/bath/ears & there's roadworks fuckin everywhere all thro adamsdown right outside my window all for the sake of beaming an extra thousand channels to me screen. there is nothing in life can shift me arse as fast as roadworks & a cold tub of water to sleep in/the remnants of hallucinogens losing their power/my vision flicks between grey & colour (the vision of the killer burnt on the victim's retina/in my eyes there are admissions to no thought bar silence & sleep).

blue sky outa bah throom window

it ties me. this inability to tell real from reality, i know what i think i know but the real leaves me panicky (rapid fade to black&white...)

(luck? what did i do with it? i did what most would do: i pisst it up against the wall) & now i know i recognise the meaning of life as survival, i don't like but who the fuck askt for my opinion...

& all i can think of is smashing thro windscreens.

....

look forward to a 4.30 breakfast at tony's/a wet salty yoke of a satdee morning delayed til the afternoon if i'm sharp before football (finalscores, not kickoff); look forward to the earlymorn knock of godbotherers come sunday (satdee written

off, all i'll do today is smoke, shit & coff stuff up) i'll burn their
fuckin ears off if they ever come near me but

i refuse to accept my social limitations
i refuse to be tied to being only one person
i am a myriad a myriad my raid a myriad
i am
    dj tabloyd
    (aka cohort for uncle weirdness & the defenders of dublov)
i am
    el throbbo
    (*i thank yaow*; & all derivatives of)
i am
    nifty leftwinger too fuckt to run
i am
    sensitive poet & occasional cunt
i am
    experienced in champagne & swimming pools
    dolequeue headslum fodder thug
i am
    model employee
    for the first two months
i am
    fotograb
    donut maker *par excellence*
i am
    (button up)
i am
    memories of dream & escapee from nitemare
    somebody's visible friend (speak only in private)
i am
    creator
    offspring
i am

(who begat *who came from* isn't up for the task)

cardiff cut

i am
    brother
i am
    AX10
i am
    card carrying member
    rep for the union
    (subs up lad)

        ('it is better for a man to conquer himself
        than for a king to conquer & capture many cities')

i am
    spokesman for myself alone
    (myself meself MESLEF: *a union of one)*

        '1001 questions to ask of your city'

& i have none.

    ....

       grasp nettle.

            find myself

                    no longer

            compliant

sick from the taste of tobacco

&
i feel like
feeling

freeform

or

i feel like
feel like
freeform

or

i feel like feeling
freefall

or

i feel like feeling
feel like feeling feel like feel like feel like feeling like feeling
feel in freefall
feel like freefall

(*i gotta turn the tape ove*
rrrrrrrrrrrrrrrrrrrrrrrrrrrrrrrrrrrrrrrrrrrrrrrrrrrrrrrrrrrrrrrrrrrrrrrrrrrrrrrrrrr
or so people tell me)

& what's this?
you may ask yourself/ask me when the sun is up
i need some distance to crash out
(it is already)

(the great celtic *what goes around comes around* research
grant juss ran out/sponsored by the donut makers of cardiff)

the crash bang wallop of intentions
the *uh, u wat?* of shortterm memory problems
the miniature microdot of truth

cardiff cut

'poetry: the oil of the universe'

bending it in

(sometimes i hafta disappear off the face of the earth,
sometimes for years)

& the splash awake

& by the time we see the sky it's already out of date

(*aark at that!*
there were priests on *strike it lucky* tonite!)

& *sim city* sez it's time to build a powerstat
& *syndicate* sez it's time to assassinate

the world is yours is yours is yours

'it takes courage to enjoy'

(energy: *nothing!* without structure).

....

i stopt learning when i began taking sides
(doan wanna make excuses i was multisubstanced at the time)

my increasing hard colon & soft underbelly
i see all this in the water around me

asea on the float of tea & fags
living on the hoof /
    off the cuff

i see all this in a cold cup

(how do i feel?
like i wanna stop my mouth a month...)

aetiology

splenetic *tang*

(i can hear myself)

phazed & dysfluent

(i may have to go visit
my homelands)

life is

'cashflow & lifestyle'
(charm is a con)

(drowns in a steamd human chillum bong)

(fadeout

cardiff cut

at long

laaasst...)

bout an hour til the day goes
completely titsup.

at the fagend of nite
the matchhead of morning
wake me when danger of going home AWOL
ring a vague bell

'stuckup to glory'

the earth

coming down

on itself

turns

something chronic

continues to

mel

&

(i am

silent...)

gerge

(cut kahdiff).

cardiff cut

for chris torrance.
big thanks.

glossary

for those interested, here's a glossary of found lines & references:

westgate hotel, john frost square
the westgate was the scene of a nineteenth century chartist riot between workers & army. the chartists were led by the englishman john frost, amongst others.

devonport royal dockyard
a train, named after the naval dockyard in plymouth where sal's father worked. the work gave him asbestosis.

thermovitrine
brand of glass used in train windows.

the cardiff giant
in 1869 the petrified remains of a man over ten feet tall were discovered under a field outside cardiff, new york state. they created a storm of interest. even after they were declared a hoax people continued to pay to view the remains. the giant, a gypsum statue, was still used as a money-making sideshow as late as the 1930's.

cariad
welsh equivalent of 'love', '(my) love', 'lover'.

dame edna
reference to the australian drag character dame edna everage & her trademark prop: a bunch of gladioli.

please release me let me go / i don't want you anymore
from the song 'release me' by engelbert humperdinck.

semolina pilchard
from the song 'i am the walrus' by the beatles (lennon/
mccartney).

yasoo
greek equivalent of 'iya' or 'seeya'.

harry secombe
a bus, named after the welsh entertainer.

*this is your life, the tomorrow people, mister benn, mister
bean, sesame street, the learning zone, strike it lucky*
tv programmes.

kampai
japanese equivalent of 'cheers'.

polizia
italian equivalent of 'police'.

efkaresto
greek equivalent of 'thank you'.

tschüß
german equivalent of 'tara', 'bye', etc.

CID
police criminal investigation department.

it's brains you want / never forget your (you're) welsh
advertising slogans for welsh beers.

the city of the grateful knights
reference to 1920s cardiff made by dr. john davies, historian.

cardiff cut

like putting your hands in a bees' hive
how george thomas, viscount tonypandy of rhonndda, described making his suggestion to the welsh parliamentary party that they put down a motion for the government to declare cardiff capital of wales.

& now my life has changed in oh so many ways / my independence seems to vanish in the haze
from the song 'help' by the beatles (lennon/mccartney).

famagusta
town in east cyprus deserted by the greek cypriot population following the turkish invasion of 1974. the turkish federated state of northern cyprus remains officially unrecognised by the UN.

jack
affectionate term for anyone from swansea.

clwb
welsh equivalent of 'club'.

mArkzies (marks & spencers), costcutter, phantasia, mister minit, woolies (woolworths)
shop names.

8track
1970's audio tape cassette system.

bookem dano!
reference to 'hawaii five-0' tv programme.

GUM
genito-urinary medicine clinic.

tracey island
reference to 'thunderbirds' tv programme.

CRI
cardiff royal infirmary.

A&E
accident & emergency department.

A
acid tab, or in this case acid microdot.

sut mae
welsh equivalent of 'how are things', 'how do', etc.

norman bates
reference to the actor anthony perkins who played bates in the hitchcock film 'psycho'.

makaton
a form of sign language.

kermit's nephew
reference to the song 'half way down the stairs' from 'the muppet show' tv programme (henson associates inc).

hola
spanish equivalent of 'hello'.

dim
welsh equivalent of 'no' (in this context, but also 'nil' 'nothing' 'anything' etc).

playstat
sony playstation games console.

cardiff cut

love me tender
song by elvis (matson, presley).

redafuckindair
a famous fuckin fireman.

made it ma, i'm top of the world!
from the film 'white heat' starring james cagney (warner bros.).

1001 questions to ask of your city
from the poem '1001 questions to ask of any city' by graham hartill.

who walkedst the foaming deep
from the hymn 'for those in peril on the sea' by william whiting.

WDA
welsh development agency.

wile e. coyote
cartoon character, falls off cliffs (warner bros.).

maxwell, murdoch, berlusconi
three of the world's biggest media tycoons; three men who, i'm sure, worked hard to uphold the freedom & impartiality of the media whilst providing much needed work for many, including lawyers.

SCFC
swansea city football club. but i support cardiff city. just thought i should put that straight.

stations of the cross
a ceremony of devotion performed before a series of images representing jesus' route to calvary.

SLR
self loading rifle.

taceval & alert states (black alpha, bikini red)
terms used to grade degrees of perceived necessary military vigilance. taceval (tactical evaluation) state refers to artifical situations such as war games. alert state refers to reality. (black alpha: normal vigilance. bikini red: a higher state of vigilance denoting a perceived threat to that specific environment).

DS
police drug squad.

trinitron
1970's sony television set.

glassbottle / bottleglass
reference to a classic line by comedian tommy cooper.

he's coming round! / thinkin: this is madness iz madness
from the poem 'crash poems: newent' by lloyd robson.

truth is molten
from the song 'goo goo barabajagal' by donovan & jeff beck (leitch).

peerless jim
peerless jim driscoll (1880-1925), cardiff boxer & local hero; undefeated welsh, british & european featherweight champion.

lynette white, geraldine palk, lily volpert
three women murdered in cardiff; three murders unsolved. in 1990 three butetown men were wronly jailed for the 1988 murder of lynette white - after each serving four years they were cleared of the charge. in 1990 geraldine palk was stabbed

over eighty times - by 2000 her killer had still not been found. in june 2001, after cardiff cut had been written, south wales police finally arrested a suspect. at the time the book went to press the case had not gone to trial. in 1952 an adamsdown man was found guilty of the murder of lily volpert & became the last person legally hanged in cardiff prison - his conviction was posthumously quashed in 1998.

cymraeg
the welsh language.

AX10
brother AX10 electronic typewriter, as used by the author.

it is better for a man to conquer himself than for a king to conquer & capture many cities
from the song 'i'm a levi' by ijahman.

poetry: the oil of the universe
from a conversation between lloyd robson & chris torrance.

sim city, syndicate
computer games loosely based on societal domination.

it takes courage to enjoy
from the song 'big time sensuality' by björk.

cashflow & lifestyle
from a conversation between lloyd robson & rachel ward.

brandnames mentioned include *armani, kickers, yves saint laurent, ellesse, adidas, levi's* (clothing); *tia maria, sambuca, bailey's, brains, welsh, keo, hooch* (alcohol); *gold v (golden virginia), rizla, sobranie* (tobacco & associated products); *bic, biro, blutak* (stationery); *mills&boon, studynotes, marvel comics* (reading material); *austin maxi, allegro, mercedes, ford, sierra* (cars); *TNT* (parcel delivery); *freightliner* (cargo transport); *ikea & habitat* (furniture); *JCB* (plant vehicles); *yale* (locks & keys); *felix* (cat food); *PG tips* & the character *mr. shifter* (teabags), & last but not least *nurofen* (over-the-counter painkiller tablets).

i reckon everything else can be found in a bogstandard dictionary, is self-evident or common knowledge, but while i'm at it: the tommy steele quote is genuine & the welsh for 'taxi' is 'tacsi'.

safe trip home.

lloyd

acknowledgements

extracts from cardiff cut were first published by blackhat smallpress & poetry wales magazine.

extracts from cardiff cut were first performed by lloyd robson for sampler: (www.sampler-poetry.freeuk.com), wired @ dempsey's, & the academi bay lit festival (www.academi.org).

thanks to sal, chris torrance, parthian, liz veasey @ bbc tv wales archive, alan & joe @ alan walsh reprographic, mike franks, paul osbourne, & everyone who appears in cardiff cut - christ knows there's enuff of you.

& to me mam.

& to me dad.

also by lloyd robson:

letter from sissi
prose poem, isbn: 0 9524251 73, £6.50

a love poem wrapt ina social reflection
wrapt ina letta home from a beautiful holiday destination
checkt out to escape shithouse 90s britain.
why come back?

"as if derek hatton has his foot in the door reciting a homage to
ginsberg" - victor golightly, new welsh review

"irreverent, hilarious, refreshingly strong - a real peach, buy it"
- steve spence, scene magazine

"vigorous & exhilarating, robson is unignorable"
- robert minhinnick, poetry wales

"the first ever cardiff dialect prose" - tôpher mills

edge territory
poetry, isbn: 0 9524251 81, £4.75

"this is so successful it's over-the-top - inspiration unites
subject & form, robson makes it look easy"
- tim allen, terrible work

"the most innovative book of the year"
- peter finch, buzz

hand-finished books from:
blackhat
40 ruby st, cardiff, wales, CF24 1LN

cheques payable to 'blackhat'